DISCOVER AMERICA

ALABAMA

Janice Parker

www.av2books.com

AV² provides enriched content that supplements and complements this book. Weigl's AV² books strive to create inspired learning and engage young minds in a total learning experience.

Your AV² Media Enhanced books come alive with...

Audio
Listen to sections of the book read aloud.

Key Words
Study vocabulary, and complete a matching word activity.

Video
Watch informative video clips.

Quizzes
Test your knowledge.

Embedded Weblinks
Gain additional information for research.

Slide Show
View images and captions, and prepare a presentation.

Try This!
Complete activities and hands-on experiments.

... and much, much more!

Go to **www.av2books.com**, and enter this book's unique code.

BOOK CODE

Y 6 7 3 3 2 8

AV² by Weigl brings you media enhanced books that support active learning.

Published by AV² by Weigl
350 5th Avenue, 59th Floor
New York, NY 10118
Website: www.av2books.com

Library of Congress Cataloging-in-Publication Data
Names: Parker, Janice, author.
Title: Alabama : the Heart of Dixie / Janice Parker.
Description: New York, NY : AV2 by Weigl, [2016] | Series: Discover America | Includes index.
Identifiers: LCCN 2015043888 (print) | LCCN 2015044979 (ebook) | ISBN 9781489648150 (hard cover : alk. paper) | ISBN 9781489648167 (soft cover : alk. paper) | ISBN 9781489648174 (Multi-User eBook)
Subjects: LCSH: Alabama--Juvenile literature.
Classification: LCC F326.3 .P373 2016 (print) | LCC F326.3 (ebook) | DDC 976.1--dc23
LC record available at http://lccn.loc.gov/2015043888

Printed in the United States of America in Brainerd, Minnesota
1 2 3 4 5 6 7 8 9 20 19 18 17 16

042016
040816

Project Coordinator Heather Kissock
Art Director Terry Paulhus

Photo Credits
Every reasonable effort has been made to trace ownership and to obtain permission to reprint copyright material. The publisher would be pleased to have any errors or omissions brought to their attention so that they may be corrected in subsequent printings. The publisher acknowledges Getty Images, Corbis Images, iStock, and Alamy as its primary image suppliers for this title.

ALABAMA

Contents

STATE TREE
Southern Longleaf Pine

STATE BIRD
Yellowhammer

STATE FLAG
Alabama

STATE FLOWER
Camillia

STATE MAMMAL
Black Bear

STATE SEAL
Alabama

Motto
Audemus Jura Nostra Defendere
(We Dare Maintain Our Rights)

Song
"Alabama," words by
Julia S. Tutwiler and music
by Edna Gockel Gussen

Population
(2010 Census) 4,779,736
Ranked 23rd state

Entered the Union
December 14, 1819, as the 22nd state

Capital
Montgomery

Discover Alabama

Alabama is a state that has amazing places and friendly people. The landscape offers a beautiful mix of vast forests, sandy coastal plains, and bountiful farmlands. Not only does Alabama border Tennessee, Georgia, Florida, and Mississippi, but this state is also located on the Gulf of Mexico.

The land has always played an important role in Alabama's economy. The state once depended mostly upon the cotton industry, but over the years, agriculture has expanded into other areas. Today Alabama produces a wide variety of crops, such as soybeans, peanuts, and melons.

Alabama has a great many natural resources that provide the state with sources of income. Alabama's abundance of natural resources provides the state with many economic opportunities. There are valuable minerals in the ground, and the rivers offer easy-access transportation routes and can produce **hydroelectricity**.

Alabama lies at the southern end of the Appalachian Mountains, which extend down through the northeastern part of the state. The mountains cover nearly half of the state. In the north is the fertile agricultural valley of the Tennessee River. Prairie lowlands south of that area hold rich farmland, where cotton was once the main crop. Farther south stretch huge forests of pine and hardwood trees. While Alabama has only 53 miles of coast, it is famous for white sand beaches.

The Land

Alabama does not have an **official nickname**, but it is known by many as "**The Heart of Dixie**."

Alabama boasts the **longest** state constitution in the U.S., with more than **100,000 words** and **700 amendments**.

Beginnings

Alabama was the starting point for both the Civil War and the civil rights movement. The state played an important role in the creation of the Confederate States of America, which was formed by the 11 Southern states that **seceded** from the rest of the country. Montgomery, known as the Cradle of the Confederacy, became the first capital of the Confederacy. In April 1861 in Montgomery, Confederate General P. G. T. Beauregard gave the order to fire on Fort Sumter, a Union fort off the coast of South Carolina. This attack was the first battle in the Civil War between the Confederacy and the Union.

Though the Civil War brought slavery to an end, African Americans continued to suffer from discrimination. In the mid-twentieth century, the civil rights movement in Alabama gained strength as African Americans struggled for freedom and equality. In 1955, Rosa Parks sent a powerful message when she refused to give up her seat on a city bus in Montgomery. At the time, Alabama law said that African Americans had to give up their seats to Caucasians. When Parks was arrested, a local activist, minister Martin Luther King, Jr., led a **boycott** of Montgomery buses. The boycott was one of the first steps on the road to **desegregation** and equal rights for African Americans.

King led the Montgomery Improvement Association to boycott the transit system and strive for civil rights.

Where is
ALABAMA?

Alabama is a nearly-square state, with straight lines making up most of its borders. In southeastern Alabama, however, the winding Chattahoochee River forms nearly half of the eastern border. In the northwest tip of the state, the Tennessee River forms a small part of the border. In the southwest, the western edge of the Florida panhandle is not a straight line. The panhandle juts into the state and separates most of southern Alabama from the Gulf of Mexico.

United States Map

Alabama

Alaska Hawai'i

MAP LEGEND

- ■ Alabama
- ☆ Capital City
- ● Major Cities
- ▧ Cathedral Caverns State Park
- ▢ Bordering States
- ▢ Water

MISSISSIPPI

N

SCALE 0 ⊢———————⊣ 50 miles

1 Montgomery

Montgomery is not only the center of state government, it is also full of history and charming architecture. Jefferson Davis took his oath as the president of the Confederacy in the state capitol building in 1861. The Lower Commerce Street Historic District showcases Victorian buildings from the 1880s to the early 1900s.

2 Birmingham

Birmingham is called the "Cradle of the Civil Rights movement." It is also the largest city in Alabama, home to 22 percent of the state's total population. Today, Birmingham is a center for medical research, banking, and public service. The city also features more green space than any other major city in the nation.

GEORGIA

Birmingham

ALABAMA

Montgomery

Mobile

FLORIDA

Gulf of Mexico

3 Cathedral Caverns

Cathedral Caverns State Park opened to the public in the summer of 2000 after it was sold to the state by a private owner. The highlight of the park are the caverns themselves. They feature an entrance that stretches 126 feet across and 25 feet high, and one of the largest **stalagmites** in the world.

4 Mobile

Mobile is Alabama's oldest city and features a rich heritage. With more than 150 historic buildings, Mobile is also a hub for notable architecture. Home to the USS *Alabama* battleship, the Port of Mobile remains the economic center of the city.

Land Features

Alabama is made up of five natural regions. Three of these regions are the Appalachian Plateau, the Piedmont Plateau, and the Ridge and Valley region. Together, the three make up the Appalachian Highlands. The Appalachian Plateau includes the southern part of the Appalachian Mountain range.

The Interior Low Plateau, in the northwestern corner of the state, has excellent farmland. The Gulf Coastal Plain is the largest region in Alabama and contains an area called the Black Belt. Named for its fertile soil, the Black Belt is known for its agriculture. The area is also a source of lumber.

Cheaha Mountain

The highest point in Alabama is Cheaha Mountain, near Talladega, at 2,407 feet.

Appalachian Plateau

The Sequoyah Caverns are located in northeastern Alabama. With their underground lakes and pools, the Sequoyah Caverns were formed over millions of years.

Interior Low Plateau

The Tennessee River flows through the northern part of Alabama.

Gulf Coastal Plain

The Alabama River flows almost completely within the Gulf Coastal Plain.

Climate

Alabama has short, mild winters and long, warm summers. Winter temperatures range from 44° to 57° Fahrenheit. In the summer, average temperatures are in the mid-1980s.

Although the climate in Alabama is usually temperate, the state can experience extreme weather. Alabama receives heavy rainfall, and hurricanes occasionally strike the Gulf Coast. Destructive tornadoes sometimes sweep across parts of the state. The highest temperature ever recorded was 112° F, reached on September 5, 1925, in Centerville. On January 30, 1966, Alabama's temperature dipped to its lowest point ever, –27° F at New Market.

Average Annual Precipitation Across Alabama

Cities in different parts of Alabama typically receive different amounts of rainfall over the course of a year. Why might Mobile get the highest amount of precipitation?

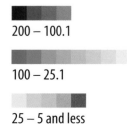

LEGEND

Average Annual Precipitation (in inches) 1961–1990

200 – 100.1

100 – 25.1

25 – 5 and less

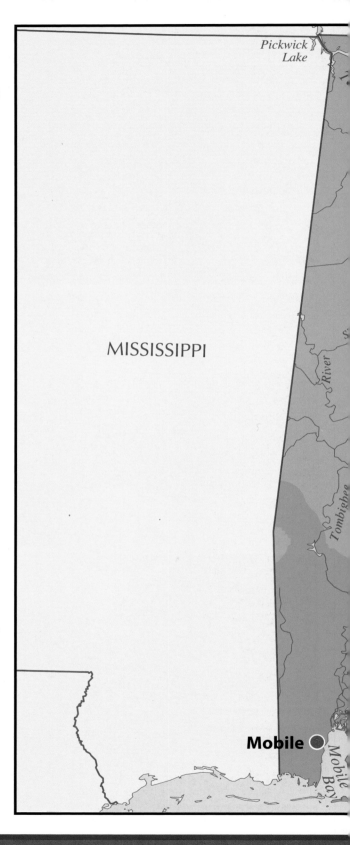

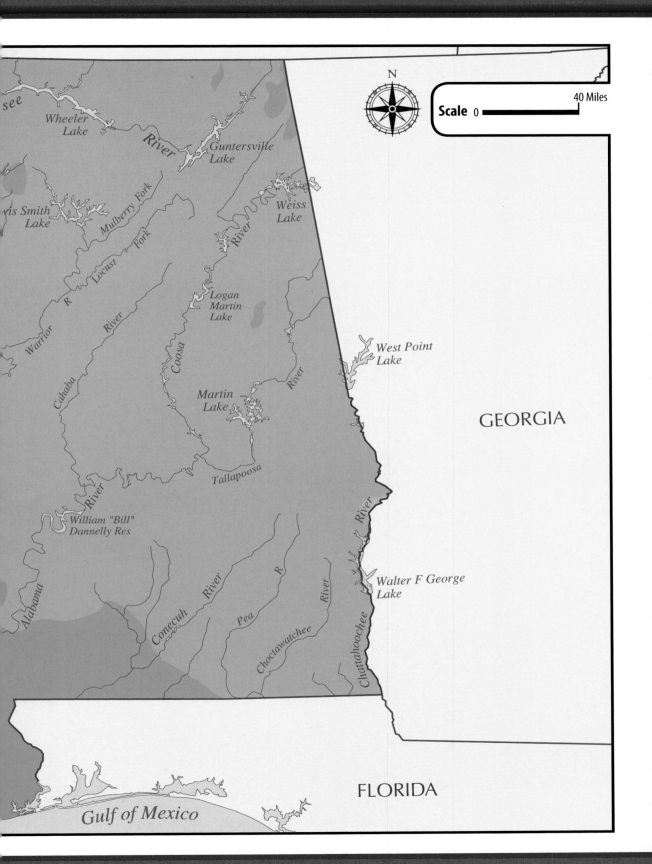

Wheeler
Lake

see

River

Guntersville
Lake

vis Smith
Lake

Mulberry Fork

Weiss
Lake

Locust Fork

River

Warrior

R

Locust

River

Logan
Martin
Lake

Cahaba

River

Coosa

River

Martin
Lake

River

West Point
Lake

N

GEORGIA

Tallapoosa

William "Bill"
Dannelly Res

Alabama

River

Conecuh

River

Pea

R

River

Choctawatchee

Walter F George
Lake

Chattahoochee

River

FLORIDA

Gulf of Mexico

Nature's Resources

Alabama has a variety of natural resources. Forests cover about two-thirds of the state. Fertile soils, a long growing season, and abundant rainfall are key to the state's agriculture. Alabama is rich in coal, limestone, **bauxite**, and white marble. The abundance of iron ore, or hematite, has contributed to the successful iron and steel industries in the state. Natural gas is one of the most valuable resources in Alabama. It accounts for more than one-half of the state's income from **fossil fuels**.

Since 1979, off-shore oil rigs have been operating off the coast of Alabama.

Alabama's rivers provide water for **irrigation** and recreation. Hydroelectricity is generated at several dams, including Muscle Shoals. The beauty of Alabama's landscape is a valuable resource, too. Wildlife preserves, trees, flowers, and caves help bring billions of tourist dollars into the state each year.

Hematite is Alabama's official state mineral.

Alabama's fertile soils produce 150,000 acres of soybeans annually.

Vegetation

More than 125 species of tree can be found in Alabama. Pine and oak trees grow throughout the state. Black walnut and sweet gum trees are plentiful. Spanish moss grows on many of the state's trees. Alabama has many flowering trees and shrubs, including magnolia, azalea, dogwood, and rhododendron. Common wildflowers, such as thistle, trillium, and prairie clover, add a splash of color to the landscape. Mistletoe, blackberries, huckleberries, and mountain laurels all grow throughout the state.

In 1992, Alabama created the Forever Wild Land Trust, which is devoted to protecting natural green spaces for many generations to come. The fund purchases tracts of land that are preserved for outdoor recreation and research. About 600,000 acres of submerged land is also protected by the trust. This includes coastal land that is up to three miles offshore.

Trillium

Trilliums grow in shady woodlands as well as in cultivated wildflower gardens. They are one of the first flowers of spring.

Oak Trees

Live oak trees line the streets of many towns in Alabama. They can grow as tall as 50 feet.

Bamboo

One of the fastest-growing plants on Earth, bamboo are tall, treelike grasses. Their woody stems can be used for flooring, food, and Chinese medicine.

Spanish Moss

Spanish moss often grows on cypress trees and southern live oaks. It looks like a long, silvery beard dripping from tree branches.

Wildlife

Alabama's forests contain bobcats, red and gray foxes, raccoons, squirrels, weasels, otters, and opossums. There are fewer larger mammals in the state, though black bears can be found in the south, and white-tailed deer in the west. Bird-watchers look for bald eagles, ospreys, brown pelicans, bluebirds, and great blue herons, among others.

Bass, trout, and catfish swim in Alabama's lakes and rivers. Mullets, red snappers, crabs, oysters, and shrimps live in the waters off the Gulf Coast. Alligators hunt their prey in swamps in the southern part of the state. Thousands of alligators live in the Mobile Delta area. Many poisonous snakes are found in Alabama. These include rattlesnakes, coral snakes, and water moccasins.

Blue Crab

Blue crabs live on muddy shores, bays, and estuaries. They can grow to 9 inches long and turn red-orange when cooked.

American Alligator

The American alligator, the only member of the crocodile family found in Alabama, lives mostly in the freshwater coastal plains. It can also be found in the cooler waters of Alabama's interior.

Armadillo

The nine-banded armadillo is the only armadillo subspecies in Alabama. Thick scales cover its head and tail, while a shell made of horn and bone protects its back.

Great Horned Owl

The great horned owl grows to more than 2 feet long. It feeds on small rodents and birds.

Economy

United States Space and Rocket Center in Huntsville

The United States Space and Rocket Center in Huntsville is one of the world's largest space-travel attraction. The center has more than 1,500 space artifacts on display and hosts one of NASA's Space Camps. At space camp, children can live like astronauts, experience weightlessness in the Gravity Trainer, eat freeze-dried food, and get the feel for flying in jet-fighter simulators.

Tourism

Tourism is an important business in Alabama. In 2010, nearly 23 million people visited the state and spent more than $9 billion. Visitors come to Alabama to enjoy the warm southern climate. Fishing, boating, and other water activities are popular in the state's lakes, rivers, and reservoirs. The Gulf of Mexico is well known as a place for ocean fishing.

The caves and caverns in the northeastern part of Alabama are also popular with tourists. The state has more than 3,000 known caves, making it an ideal spot for **spelunking**. The limestone in Rickwood Caverns is believed to be more than 260 million years old.

Rosa Parks Library and Museum

The Rosa Parks Library and Museum is rated the number one tourist location in Montgomery.

Birmingham Botanical Gardens

The Birmingham Botanical Gardens contain more than 10,000 different plants growing in more than 25 different gardens. Beautiful sculptures dot the grounds.

McWane Science Center

The McWane Science Center contains four floors of exhibits, including several on dinosaurs, as well as laser and light exhibits. The aquarium includes a shark and ray touch tank.

In 2014, Alabama landed more than 25 million pounds of gulf coast shrimp.

Primary Industries

Fishing is a multimillion-dollar industry in Alabama. The state has both freshwater and saltwater commercial fishing. Shrimp are the most valuable saltwater seafood. Oysters, blue crab, and red snapper are also important. Buffalo fish, mussels, and catfish are caught in freshwater streams.

Mineral resources are abundant in Alabama, and mining is very important to the state's economy. The underground coal mines in western Alabama are some of the deepest in the nation. White marble, most often used in paper pigments, and limestone are also major resources for the state.

The production of iron and steel, in the Birmingham area, is one of the main industries in Alabama. Steel production occurs mostly in Birmingham, Decatur, and Gadsden. **Fabricated metals**, such as cast-iron pipes and metal valves, are also made in the region.

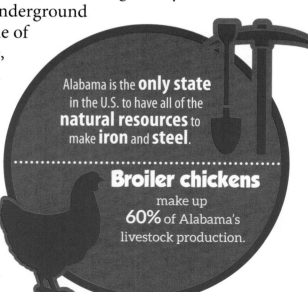

Alabama is the **only state** in the U.S. to have all of the **natural resources** to make **iron** and **steel**.

Broiler chickens make up **60%** of Alabama's livestock production.

Value of Goods and Services (in Millions of Dollars)

Alabama is known for being a place where businesses can thrive. It has a good workforce-training program, plenty of natural resources, a good climate for agriculture, and vast forest lands. There will likely be a large increase in jobs in the healthcare industry over the next twenty years. Why do you think that might be?

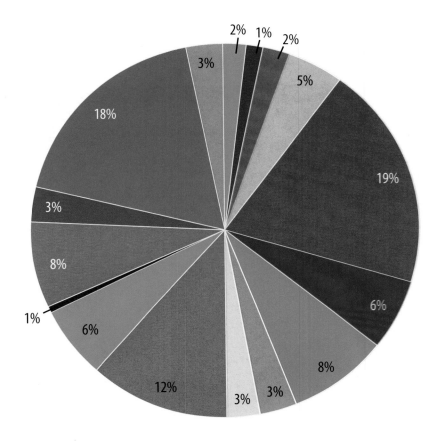

Agriculture, Forestry, Fishing	$14,347	Media & Entertainment	$19,191
Mining	$10,688	Finance, Insurance & Real Estate	$85,486
Utilities	$16,824	Professional & Business Services	$43,295
Construction	$33,010	Education	$4,287
Manufacturing	$141,333	Health Care & Social Services	$54,701
Wholesale Trade	$44,847	Hotels & Restaurants	$21,955
Retail Trade	$60,019	Government	$130,906
Transportation & Warehousing	$23,120	Other Services	$21,445

Goods and Services

Cotton was once Alabama's most important product. The invasion of the **boll weevil** in 1915 destroyed a large portion of the state's cotton crops. This forced farmers to make changes and raise other crops. Corn and soybeans are grown in the southern part of Alabama. Peanuts, pecans, hay, oats, tobacco, and wheat are other important crops. The state also produces many fruits and vegetables, including peaches, apples, watermelons, beans, potatoes, and sweet potatoes.

Nearly half of the peanuts grown in the United States come from Alabama.

Huntsville is known for its production of missiles. Alabama workers built the rocket that took humans to the Moon. The Marshall Space Flight Center, in Huntsville, is where NASA conducts rocket tests and trains astronauts.

Alabama has been fabricating steel since the nineteenth century.

The pulp and paper industry is another valuable source of income for Alabama. It includes the producers of sanitary paper products, box manufacturers, and pulp and paper mills. Chemical manufacturers in Alabama produce paint, fertilizer, and varnish. **Textile** mills, lumber mills, meatpacking plants, and industrial-machinery factories are also important.

Alabama's waterways help the state transport raw materials and finished products. Ships deliver goods to the state and unload them at the Alabama State Docks in Mobile Bay. The Alabama State Docks operates a system of about 30 general cargo berths and about 4 million square feet of storage space. The ships transport coal, iron, steel, petroleum products, pulp and other wood products, soybeans, and wheat.

Barges on Alabama's waterways transport goods throughout the state and play an important role in the economy.

History

The Moundville Archaeological Park has preserved the remains of an ancient village dating back to 1000 AD.

Native Americans

Archaeological sites reveal that people lived on the land that is now Alabama as early as 10,000 years ago. These early peoples were hunters who used caves for shelter. By about 1000 BC, they had begun to plant crops and build permanent settlements. Later, they lived in villages built around large mounds of earth. The mounds were an important part of their culture. These early inhabitants are sometimes called the Mound Builders.

Soon after the time of the Mound Builders, other groups of Native Americans began to settle the Alabama area. By the 1700s, four major Native American nations were living in the region. They were the Cherokees, the Creeks, the Choctaws, and the Chickasaws. By the late 1830s, the United States government had forced these groups to move from their homes in Alabama to reservations in Oklahoma to make room for Caucasian settlers. Despite the upheaval and deaths caused by these changes, the move west did not extinguish these tribes. All these tribes have thriving cultures today.

By 1800, most Cherokees lived on farmsteads in northeast Alabama and had established communities. These communities provided structure and gave rise to strong leadership within the Cherokee Nation.

Exploring the Land

The first Europeans to reach the Alabama area were Spanish explorers. This group included Alonso Alvarez de Piñeda, who sailed into Mobile Bay in 1519. Around 1540, Spaniard Hernando de Soto and his army moved up from the Gulf of Mexico in search of gold. He raided Native American villages, took hostages, and tortured Native Americans for information and for food. De Soto's treatment of Native Americans resulted in many conflicts. One of the worst of these battles was with Chief Tuscaloosa at Maubila, or Mobile. The battle resulted in the deaths of several thousand Native Americans and left De Soto's troops severely weakened.

Timeline of Settlement

1702 France founds the first permanent European settlement in Alabama, Fort Louis.

First European Settlements

1717 Fort Toulouse is built on the Coosa River to encourage trade with the Native Americans and reduce the influence of the British.

1689 French explorers claim the Mississippi River Basin for France.

1763 France **cedes** territorial claims east of the Mississippi River, including Alabama, to Great Britain, as part of the terms to end the French and Indian War.

1519 Spanish explorers arrive at what is now Mobile Bay.

Early Exploration

In 1559, Don Tristán de Luna traveled from Mexico to Mobile, with 500 soldiers and 1,000 colonists, to start a settlement. The group also looked unsuccessfully for gold. In 1561, a fierce storm destroyed much of their food and supplies, forcing them to return to Mexico.

For the next 250 years, the French, British, and Spanish struggled for control of the area. Each group tried to make alliances with Native American tribes living there. Eventually initial control was granted to the French.

1813 The United States claims Mobile from Spain.

1819 Alabama becomes the 22nd state.

1830s Creek Indians are illegally removed from their homelands in Alabama and forced to move to Oklahoma.

1861 Alabama secedes from the United States and joins the Confederate States of America.

1783 The Treaty of Paris, which formally ends the American Revolution, gives Mobile to Spain and the rest of Alabama to the newly created United States of America.

1868 Alabama ratifies a new state constitution that protects the civil rights of African Americans and is allowed back into the Union as a state.

American Revolution and Civil War

The First Settlers

In 1702, French-Canadian explorer Jean-Baptiste Le Moyne, sieur de Bienville, established a French settlement on the Mobile River. After a flood, the settlement was moved to the site of present-day Mobile and renamed Fort Condé de la Mobile. The fort was the center of the French government for the Louisiana colony during the early 1700s.

Soon, settlers began to arrive from France and Canada. Early French settlers nearly starved to death waiting for supply ships to arrive from France. In 1719, the French brought slaves over from Africa to clear fields and harvest crops.

Jean-Baptiste Le Moyne, sieur de Bienville, also founded what is now New Orleans, Louisiana.

Slave labor fueled the cotton plantations of Alabama until the end of the Civil War.

In 1763, France gave up almost all its territory in North America east of the Mississippi River to Great Britain. When the American Revolution ended in 1783, northern Alabama became part of the United States, while Mobile and southern Alabama were ruled by Spain. The United States purchased Mobile from the Spanish, and in 1817, Alabama became a territory of the United States.

Settlers soon moved into the Alabama territory to take advantage of its fertile land. By 1819, enough people lived in the territory to qualify it for statehood. Alabama joined the Union on December 14, 1819.

Jefferson Davis was inaugurated on Feb. 18, 1861, as the first and only president of the Confederate States.

History Makers

Many notable Alabamans contributed to the development of their state, their nation, and the world. They came from all walks of life and many different cultures. They include the original Native American inhabitants, European American settlers and politicians, and African American activists.

Sequoyah (c. 1760-1843)

Sequoyah was the son of a Cherokee woman and a British trader. He became convinced that developing a system for writing down the oral Cherokee language would help maintain independence from European settlers. Because his 86-symbol system was simple, the ability to read and write spread rapidly among the Cherokees, and they were able to publish their own books and newspapers. The giant redwoods of northern California, called the sequoias, are named after him.

George Washington Carver (1864–1943)

George Washington Carver was born into slavery. For more than fifty years, he researched agricultural products that revolutionized agriculture in the South. He discovered hundreds of uses for peanuts, soybeans, and sweet potatoes and developed ways to extract dyes from clay soil. In 1896, Carver became the director of the Department of Agricultural Research at Tuskegee Normal and Industrial Institute, now Tuskegee University. His discoveries helped replace cotton as the main agricultural product of Alabama.

Hugo Black (1886–1971)

Born in Harlan, Hugo Black spent his early years watching court trials and political rallies, inspiring him to become a lawyer. Once elected to the U.S. Senate, Black introduced minimum-wage legislation, which became law. Appointed to the Supreme Court, he was a strong defender of everyone's right to free speech.

Ralph David Abernathy (1926–1990)

The grandchild of a slave, Ralph David Abernathy was raised on his family's large farm in Morengo County. He became a founder of the civil rights movement. Along with Martin Luther King, Jr., he helped lead the Montgomery bus boycott and founded the Southern Christian Leadership Conference, which became the most visible civil rights organization in the South.

Condoleezza Rice (1954–)

Born in Birmingham, Rice was an accomplished student and graduated from college at age 19. She was also a champion-level ice skater. Originally a college professor and then a policy adviser to government leaders, she became secretary of state for President George W. Bush from 2005 to 2009.

Culture

Auburn University opened in 1859, closed during the Civil War, and then reopened again in 1866. Today, the campus has more than 27,000 students enrolled.

The People Today

More than 4.8 million people live in Alabama. The five most populated cities in Alabama are Birmingham, Montgomery, Mobile, Huntsville, and Tuscaloosa. According to the 2010 Census, Alabama has a **population density** of more than 94 people per square mile. This is greater than the national average, which is about 87 people per square mile.

Birmingham is home to 22 percent of Alabama's total population.

According to the U.S. Census Bureau, Alabamans of European heritage made up the largest percentage of the population at 71 percent. African Americans were second at 26 percent. About 3 percent of Alabamans are Hispanic. Asian Americans and Native Americans each accounted for less than 1 percent.

Alabama has a current high school graduation rate of approximately 80 percent. Per the 2010 census, people over the age of 25 have a 31 percent high school graduation rate, while 24 percent have either a 4-year or 2-year college degree. In 2014, Alabama was the seventh poorest state in the nation, with a poverty rate of 18.7 percent. The number of African Americans living in poverty was more than twice the number of Caucasians. The state is working to promote education and jobs for low-income and homeless individuals and families.

Alabama's population **increased** by **more than 300,000** people from **2000 to 2010**.

Q What are some of the reasons that many people from other states and other countries are choosing to move to Alabama?

The Alabama state capital, located in Montgomery, was also the first Confederate capital.

State Government

Alabama is governed under its sixth constitution, which was adopted in 1901. The Alabama government is divided into three branches. They are the executive, the legislative, and the judicial branches. The governor, who is elected for a four-year term, is the head of the executive branch. The governor's main purpose is to make sure that state laws are enforced. The secretary of state, the state treasurer, and the attorney general are part of the executive branch of government.

The legislative branch is responsible for creating laws. The Alabama Legislature is made up of a House of Representatives and a Senate. Alabama has 105 state representatives and 35 state senators, all elected for four-year terms. The judicial branch includes the state Supreme Court, the court of civil appeals, and the court of criminal appeals. All judges and justices are elected for six-year terms.

The Alabama state legislature meets in the legislative chambers of the capitol building.

Robert Bentley is the 53rd Governor of the state of Alabama.

Alabama's state song is called
"Alabama."

From thy praries broad and fertile,
Where thy snow-white cotton shines.
To the hills where coal and iron
Hide in thy exhaustless mines.
Strong-armed miners, sturdy farmers:
Loyal hearts what'er we be.
Alabama, Alabama,
We will aye be true to thee!

Where the perfumed
south-wind whispers,
Thy magnolia groves among,
Softer than a mother's kisses,
Sweeter than a mother's song
Where the golden jasmine trailing,
Woos the treasure-laden bee,
Alabama, Alabama,
we will aye be true to thee!

* exerpted

The Birmingham Civil Rights Institute stands as a memorial to the civil rights movement.

Celebrating Culture

Alabama's rich culture has a strong connection to the civil rights movement of the 1950s and 1960s. The Birmingham Civil Rights District serves as an important reminder of the African American struggle for equal rights. The district occupies six city blocks and includes the Birmingham Civil Rights Institute, Kelly Ingram Park, the Carver Theater, and the 16th Street Baptist Church.

Birmingham's Fourth Avenue Business District was a major African American cultural area, similar to the neighborhoods of Harlem in New York City and Bronzeville in Chicago. It was once the location of more

The 16th St. Baptist church is a National Historic Landmark and part of the Birmingham Civil Rights District.

than 3,400 African American businesses, some of which still operate today. In the early 1900s, the segregated district was the only place where African American businesses were allowed to operate. The area thrived with restaurants, financial companies, barbershops, theaters, and nightclubs. Today, many of the buildings have been renovated as part of the historic Civil Rights District.

The Birmingham Civil Rights Institute was created in 1992 to educate people about African American culture and the fight for equality. Exhibits show what it was like for African Americans to live in a segregated society, using separate drinking fountains, going to separate schools, and attending civil rights rallies. The institute educates visitors about the struggle for equal services and equal rights.

Alabama's European cultural heritage is celebrated in the city of Mobile. The Mobile **Mardi Gras** is a combination of both French and Spanish traditions. Dozens of groups build elegant floats and parade through downtown Mobile. Mobile's first Mardi Gras parade consisted of one decorated coal wagon hitched up to a mule. Today, about 20 separate parades are held over several weeks.

Mardi Gras season in Mobile starts in November. During the last two weeks of the season, there is a parade every day.

To Kill A Mockingbird was released as a major motion picture in 1962.

Arts and Entertainment

Many important scholars and writers have come from Alabama. Helen Keller was an acclaimed author and lecturer from Tuscumbia. Keller, who was blind and deaf, became an inspiration to many by learning, despite her disabilities, to read **braille** and to speak.

The historic march from Selma to Montgomery, culminating in the signing of The Voting Rights Act of 1965, was commemorated in a 2014 movie titled *Selma*. Produced by Oprah Winfrey and directed by Ava DuVernay, the movie chronicles a three-month period in Dr. Martin Luther King Jr.'s life, as he campaigned for equal voting rights. Alabaman Harper Lee won a Pulitzer Prize for her 1960 novel *To Kill a Mockingbird*. Since its publication, *To Kill a Mockingbird* has never been out of print and is one of the most widely read books in the English language.

Heather Whitestone, born in Dothan, Alabama, was the **first Miss America** chosen with a **disability**.

With the airing of **"The Nat King Cole Show"** in 1956, Alabama native Nat King Cole was the **first African American** to host a **variety show.**

Traditional music is played throughout Alabama. Jazz, blues, gospel, country, and rock musicians from Alabama are internationally renowned. Many Alabama musicians have been inducted into the Alabama Music Hall of Fame, in Tuscumbia, as well as into the Rock and Roll Hall of Fame and Museum and into the Country Music Hall of Fame, both of which are located outside the state. They include Nat King Cole, Dinah Washington, Tammy Wynette, Hank Williams, Wilson Pickett, and The Temptations.

Born in Alabama, Channing Tatum has appeared in more than 20 films.

Hank Williams, sometimes called the Father of Modern Country Music, was born in 1923 in Mount Olive. At a time when most other country music singers performed other people's songs, Williams wrote his own music and created his own sound. He was inducted into the Country Music Hall of Fame in 1961. His son and grandson, both also named Hank, extend the family tradition of country music.

Hank Williams released 35 songs that made the Top 10 Billboard Country & Western Best Sellers list.

Alabama Crimson Tide has one of the best records in the Southeastern NCAA Conference.

Sports and Recreation

Alabamans love sports. The state has a history of producing world-class athletes. University football teams have a large and enthusiastic following. Many teams, like the University of Alabama's Crimson Tide and Auburn University's Auburn Tigers, share intense rivalries. Famous National Football League players from Alabama include Bart Starr, Joe Namath, and Ken Stabler.

Born in Leeds, **Charles Barkley** spent the majority of his career playing for the **Chicago Bulls** as a member of "The Dream Team" and is listed as one of the **NBA's all time 50 best players**.

Mia Hamm, two-time Women's World Cup **champion**, and two-time Olympic **gold medalist**, was born in Selma.

Avid golfers travel to Alabama to play the 468-hole Robert Trent Jones Golf Trail. The trail includes golf courses at 11 different locations across the state. Outdoor recreation can also be found in Alabama's 22 state parks. Families go to the parks for swimming, hiking, fishing, boating, and camping.

In baseball, Alabama produces home run hitters. Baseball legend Hank Aaron was born in Mobile in 1934. He was a professional baseball player for 23 seasons, during which he hit an amazing 755 home runs. He is also known for his quiet fight against discrimination in professional baseball. Born in Westfield in 1931, Willie Mays was the star center fielder for the New York Giants for most of his career and hit 660 home runs. Aaron and Mays are among the top home run hitters in the history of Major League Baseball.

Track and field star Jesse Owens was born in Oakville in 1913. He began to set world track and field records when he was still in high school. At the 1936 Olympic Games in Berlin, Germany, Owens won gold medals in the 100-meter dash, 200-meter dash, long jump, and 400-meter relay. At the time, German leader Adolf Hitler claimed the racist theory that all non-white, non-European peoples were inferior. By winning his four gold medals, Owens proved him wrong.

The Robert Trent Jones Golf Trail includes 11 championship-caliber golf courses across Alabama.

Jesse Owens was the first American to win four gold medals in track and field at the Olympics.

Get To Know
ALABAMA

The first 911 call
in the United States was made on Feburary 16, 1968 in Haleyville, Alabama.

ANNISTON, ALABAMA IS HOME TO THE WORLD'S LARGEST OFFICE CHAIR. IT IS MADE OF 10 TONS OF STEEL.

In 1886, Montgomery became home to the world's first **electric trolley system**.

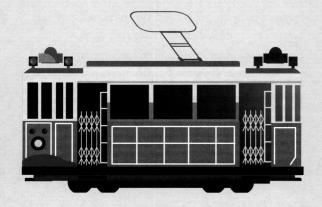

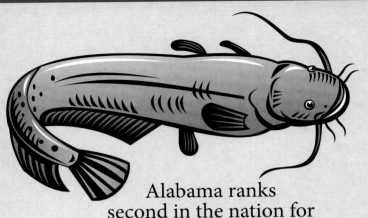

Alabama ranks second in the nation for **catfish production**, selling **$107.5 million** worth in 2010.

Alabama is the **13th largest** state in the U.S. by area.

The Birmingham Airport opened in 1931. At that time, a flight from Alabama to California took 19 hours.

The state reptile is the Alabama **RED-BELLIED TURTLE.**

Brain Teasers

What have you learned about Alabama after reading this book? Test your knowledge by answering these questions. All of the information can be found in the text you just read. The answers are provided below for easy reference.

1 What is the capital of Alabama?

2 Which body of water is next to Alabama?

3 In what year did Alabama become the 22nd state?

4 Which Alabama-born Supreme Court Justice worked to secure free speech for everyone?

5 What are the earliest known inhabitants of Alabama called?

6 How many known caves exist in Alabama?

8 What is the highest temperature ever recorded in Alabama?

7 Which important natural resource is mined in the Birmingham area?

ANSWER KEY
1. Montgomery 2. The Gulf of Mexico 3. 1819 4. Hugo Black 5. Mound Builders 6. More than 3,000 7. Iron 8. 112° F

Key Words

archaeological: related to the study of early peoples through artifacts and remains

bauxite: a clay-like rock that is the main ore in aluminum

boll weevil: a small beetle that feeds on cotton bolls, the protective case around the cotton

boycott: a refusal to purchase or participate in something as a means of protest

braille: a method of writing for the blind that uses a system of raised dots on the page

cedes: yields or grants something, usually by treaty

desegregation: the ending of legal separations and restrictions based on race

fabricated metals: metals that are manufactured

fossil fuels: fuels made from fossils, such as oil, coal, and natural gas

hydroelectricity: electricity produced using moving water

irrigation: the supplying of water to fields by means of a system of pipes, ditches, or streams

Mardi Gras: a festival whose name means "Fat Tuesday" in French, celebrated on the final Tuesday before Christian Lent

population density: the average number of people per unit of area

seceded: formally left an organization or nation

spelunking: the recreational activity of exploring caves and caverns underground

stalagmites: cone-shaped stone formations on the floors of caves

textile: a fabric made by weaving or knitting

Index

Log on to www.av2books.com

AV² by Weigl brings you media enhanced books that support active learning. Go to www.av2books.com, and enter the special code found on page 2 of this book. You will gain access to enriched and enhanced content that supplements and complements this book. Content includes video, audio, weblinks, quizzes, a slide show, and activities.

AV² Online Navigation

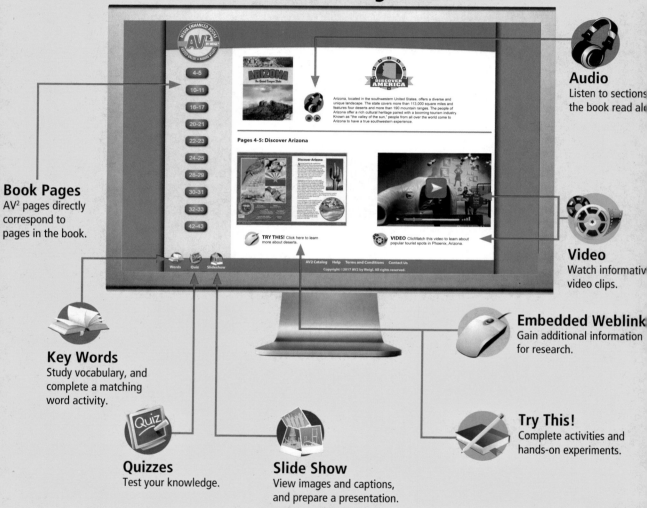

Audio
Listen to sections the book read al...

Video
Watch informativ... video clips.

Embedded Weblink...
Gain additional information for research.

Try This!
Complete activities and hands-on experiments.

Book Pages
AV² pages directly correspond to pages in the book.

Key Words
Study vocabulary, and complete a matching word activity.

Quizzes
Test your knowledge.

Slide Show
View images and captions, and prepare a presentation.

AV² was built to bridge the gap between print and digital. We encourage you to tell us what you like and what you want to see in the future.

Sign up to be an AV² Ambassador at www.av2books.com/ambassador.